SO *YOU* THINK **YOU'VE** *GOT IT* **BAD?**

A KID'S LIFE IN **ANCIENT EGYPT**

First published 2018 by Nosy Crow Ltd
The Crow's Nest, 14 Baden Place,
Crosby Row, London SE1 1YW
www.nosycrow.com

ISBN 978 1 78800 135 9

Nosy Crow and associated logos are trademarks
and/or registered trademarks of Nosy Crow Ltd.

Published in collaboration with the British Museum.

Text © Chae Strathie 2018
Illustrations © Marisa Morea 2018

A CIP catalogue record for this book is available from the British Library.

Printed in Turkey.
Papers used by Nosy Crow are made from wood
grown in sustainable forests.

135798642

SO *YOU* THINK YOU'VE GOT IT BAD?

A KID'S LIFE IN
ANCIENT
EGYPT

CONTENTS

CLOTHES AND HAIRSTYLES
Pages 6–9

FAMILY LIFE
Pages 10–15

THE HOME
Pages 16–23

CHORES AND JOBS
Pages 24–29

EDUCATION
Pages 30–33

DISCIPLINE

Pages 34–37

DIET

Pages 38–43

HEALTH AND MEDICINE

Pages 44–49

GODS, AMULETS AND PROTECTION

Pages 50–53

STILL THINK YOU'VE GOT IT BAD?

Pages 60–61

GLOSSARY

Pages 62–63

FUN AND GAMES

Pages 54–59

INDEX

Page 64

FETCH!

CLOTHES AND HAIRSTYLES

Has your dad ever made you wear a pair of trainers so terrible they make you want to hide your feet in buckets filled with concrete?

Perhaps your gran once knitted you a jumper that was **SO BRIGHT** it could be **SEEN FROM SPACE**?

Or maybe your mum took you for a haircut that left your head looking like it had been **ATTACKED BY A SQUIRREL WITH A HEDGE-TRIMMER**?

Well if you think *YOU'VE* GOT IT BAD . . . at least you actually **HAVE** clothes!

Back in ancient Egypt, children were often depicted in paintings and carvings as being **COMPLETELY** and **UTTERLY, STARK-STARING, NO-PANTS-IN-SIGHT NUDE** as the day they were born.

It's not known whether they actually did run about naked most of the time – up to the age of 12 or so – or if that was just a way of drawing them so it was clear they were kids and not adults.

Anyone got a bum-shaped woolly hat?

Given the climate of Egypt, it wouldn't be at all surprising if clothes really were an optional extra in the scorching heat of the day, although it could get pretty chilly at night and in the early morning.

You'd have to be careful — if you didn't watch out you could either get sunburn (or should that be **BUMBURN**?) or have your bottom **TURNED BLUE WITH THE COLD.**

It is also thought that during certain special occasions young servants, including slave boys and girls, walked about without clothes on — not even a pair of **NICE STRIPEY PYJAMAS** or a **STYLISH TRACKSUIT.**

However, judging by interesting finds made over the years by archaeologists, it is clear that clothes were made for children, so even if they were naked sometimes, at other times they were dressed. **PHEW!**

TA DA!

One pleated linen dress is said to be the oldest surviving item of clothing in the world at nearly 5,000 years old!

That's something to bear in mind the next time you see a pile of old clothes in a second-hand shop. That pair of **STINKY SOCKS** might have once belonged to an Egyptian pharaoh! King **TOE-TANKHAMUN**, perhaps?

7

You look lovely, dear.

I am literally never leaving my bedroom!

Some paintings — particularly from the Middle Kingdom period — show children wearing clothes copying their parents' fashions.

A dress discovered in 1982, in the tomb of a young girl called Niuty at Saqqara, has a style of skirt and separate V-shaped bodice that is the same as grown-up women wore.

Imagine wearing **EXACTLY** the same gear as your **MUM AND DAD!** Arrrggghhh! You'd never be able to leave the house! **HOW EMBARRASSING.**

FANCY THAT!

Queen Hatshepsut was shown in paintings with a beard, to show she was as powerful as a king. So if you doodle a goatee on a photo of your mum, you can get out of it by telling her it's because you think she's as great as an Egyptian queen!

But what about your head? What was going on up there in ancient Egypt?

Well, **NOT A LOT** — in the sense that most of your lovely locks would be shaved off.

That might have been a **BIT UNCOMFORTABLE** when it was cold, but on the plus side imagine the time you'd save in the shower with no hair to wash!

Ever get the feeling we should find a new barber?

Ooooh, yes.

AND HEY, GIRLS: don't think it's just the boys we're talking about. The most common hairstyle was **THE SAME FOR BOTH BOYS AND GIRLS** — either shaved bald or very short over most of the head, with a single length of braided hair hanging down the right side with the end rolled-up in an outward curl.

AT LEAST IT SAVED TIME WHEN YOU WENT FOR A HAIRCUT!

What would you like today, young man? Shaved with just a single braid of hair left over or shaved with just a single braid of hair left over?

Hmmm, I think I might go for shaved with just a single braid of hair left over this time.

EXCELLENT CHOICE!

FANCY THAT!

A dye for grey hair was made with fat from a black snake. So if your gran gets a new look, but also starts hissing at people and wriggling along the ground, now you know why.

Do you ever wish... you could get a cool new haircut?

Well, why not go all ancient Egyptian, yeah? As well as the classic "braid of hair down the side of a bald head" look, some Egyptian kids had a style that featured just three tufts of hair on top of their head. Imagine your mum's face! Some grown-ups who didn't want to be bald encouraged hair to grow on their heads by rubbing in an ointment made from the fat of snakes, crocodiles and hippos.

Wealthy Egyptians wore elaborate wigs made of human hair. It was even thought that one wig in the British Museum's collection was padded out with sheep's wool, though it was later found to be real hair. Just as well – a woolly wiggy would definitely have caused a baaa-d hair day!

Next time you're grumbling about your hairdo, just be thankful you don't stink of hippo fat!

9

FAMILY LIFE

Brothers and sisters can be a bit annoying, can't they? They're always fiddling with your stuff, or following you around, or flicking baked beans at you behind your mum's back, or, you know, just being totally brother-and-sistery.

And if you fall out with them **BIG TIME**, you'll probably be banned from playing the Xbox forever as a punishment.

But if you think *YOU'VE* GOT IT BAD, at least you don't live in an ancient Egyptian family . . .

While wealthy families had servants like nannies and maids to take care of the children, in most families the mummy did that.

Fetch me a bag of jelly mummies and a can of cola, my good man.

Yeah, good luck with that...

Of course, when we say "the mummy" we mean the mother, rather than the **CREEPY BANDAGE-WRAPPED THING**. That would not be at all comforting when it shuffled upstairs at night to tuck you in to your reed mat and read you some bedtime hieroglyphs.

Night night, sleep tight. Don't let the scorpions bite!

Egyptian women worked hard around the house, but they had almost as many rights as men, although the father headed the household. At least he couldn't hog the TV controls back then.

11

Children started to help their parents from a young age, which was awfully nice of them.

And that doesn't mean OCCASIONALLY tidying their bedroom in a half-hearted way after being nagged for A YEAR (sound familiar?)...

FANCY THAT!

King Rameses II had many wives — and over 100 children! So if you're fed up being the middle brother or sister, think yourself lucky!

So what are the chances I can go and hang out with my friends ... on a scale of zero to no chance?

Paintings from ancient Egypt show girls looking after younger brothers and sisters and, like their mothers, carrying them in a sling.

Can you imagine having to cart your little bro or sis around in a sling? How UTTERLY EMBARRASSING — SO UNCOOL, and not exactly handy when you have to carry your schoolbag, too.

NO. THANKS.

Boys had to help out the family as well. An ancient form of "schoolbook" told how a baker, when putting bread into the oven to bake, had to put his head into the oven while his son held his feet. If the boy let him slip . . . the baker fell into the bottom of the oven.

Whoops! Sorry, Dad. Pass up a doughnut while you're down there, would you?

HEEEEEEEELLLLLLPPP!!!

FANCY THAT!

To keep the royal line pure, a pharaoh might marry his own sister as his chief wife. So his mum and dad were also his parents-in-law! Eeeuw.

12

Judging by evidence from the time, it seems Egyptian kids from thousands of years ago were pretty much the same as you are today.

In the Tomb of Menna, images show two girls in a cornfield who are having a **PROPER ROW** and trying to **PULL EACH OTHER'S HAIR**. It's entirely possible they were sisters!

Mind you, below this image, another picture suggests some children were less naughty. In it one girl sits back, stretching out her bare foot while another gently examines it, perhaps trying to pull out a thorn.

Clearly **THEY** were **NOT** related.

13

Pets can be part of your family, too. It's great fun having a pet, although sometimes they can be a bit, well . . . annoying.

A cat's main method of waking you up to fetch it breakfast at 6AM is plonking its FURRY BEHIND on your face, while dogs are OBSESSED with going for walkies!

But at least most pets nowadays don't try to eat you (unless you have a particularly FEROCIOUS HAMSTER).

GAZELLE

MONKEY

FISH

The ancient Egyptians kept MONKEYS, BABOONS, FISH, GAZELLES, BIRDS and even LIONS.

But they also had pets we would recognise, too.

BIRD

BABOON

On the dog front there were domesticated ones as well as wild ones called jackals. They were members of the wolf family and looked like slim dogs with big ears. Jackals were scavengers, finding food scraps and dead animals to eat. YUCK!

Remember that next time you're grumbling about having to open a tin of dog food for your pooch.

JACKAL

DOG

LION *

CAT

Ancient Egyptians LOVED cats — in fact, they treated them almost LIKE GODS! When a cat died, its owners even SHAVED OFF THEIR EYEBROWS to show they were in mourning. Cats were also turned into mummies when they died. Or should that be "MEOW-MIES"?

* It is not known whether children really had lions as pets, but Rameses II certainly did. Best stock up on cat food then!

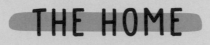

THE HOME

You might not like where you live — perhaps you have to share
a room with your brother . . .

. . . who has a snore like a JET-POWERED LAWNMOWER and produces SUSPICIOUS SMELLS
throughout the night, or maybe your neighbour practises the tuba for 12 HOURS A DAY?

But if you think *YOU'VE* GOT IT BAD . . .

At least you don't live in a house MADE OF MUD!

In ancient Egypt, pretty much **ALL** of the houses were made of mud. OK, it wasn't the gloopy kind. No, these houses were made from mud bricks that had been hardened in the sun.

Sometimes extremely wealthy people lined the outside of their homes with white limestone, which was **SUPER-PRICEY** but made the houses **GLITTER** in the sunshine.

SOUNDS SWANKY, but imagine your mum's face if you leaned against the shiny white wall with dirty hands. She'd have you down at the Nile fetching water to clean it faster than you could say "**JUMPING JACKALS!**"

Mummy likes your drawings . . . just not all over the side of her nice shiny house.

Wealthy people had porters to carry their shopping. Nowadays we just have shopping trolleys, which doesn't sound as exciting.

17

Imagine living in a place with no running water . . .

There were **NO TAPS**, so twice a day the women collected water from a well or river and filled huge clay vessels that stood by the doorway of every house.

Puff! Are you sure we didn't scoop up a hippo by mistake?

Of course, if there was no running water for taps that meant there was no running water for, errr, other stuff.

We're talking about **TOILETS**, in case you hadn't guessed.

That's right, when it was "**POO O'CLOCK**" there was no handy flush available.

Please don't trip ...
Please don't trip ...
Please don't trip ...

Unless you were rich, you had to make do with a stool with a **HOLE** in it! And underneath? Just a container filled with sand.

It's DEFINITELY your turn.

Gasp! Pass the poo mask!

Oh, slaaave ...

Wondering who's going to empty that by hand?

HELLO, YOU.

Of course, if you were wealthy, chances were you had slaves to do the dirty work.

19

What else might you find inside the typical ancient Egyptian home? Well, let's go through the front door to have a look.

Wealthy types lived in **GRAND HOMES** which had as many as **30 ROOMS**. If it was your turn to do the vacuuming it could take several months. Luckily, vacuum cleaners hadn't been invented, so it wasn't a problem.

FLAT ROOFS were used for **COOKING** or even **SLEEPING** on. In the hot climate of Egypt it was cooler up on the roof, and poorer peeps would lie on mats in the open air.

There was **NO GLASS** in the **WINDOWS**, but there were bars on them. Why? To keep the wild beasts out, of course — and we're not talking about particularly hungry moths.

21

As far as furniture went, ancient Egyptian homes didn't have much.

Stools and small tables were the most common pieces.
Flatscreen TVs and microwave ovens were **VERY RARE**.

Yes it is... if it was made by a baboon sliding backwards down a pyramid with its eyes shut.

This is the Best. Pot. Ever.

FANCY THAT!
Poorer people made their own clothes and furniture, wove mats and baskets from reeds, and made simple pots. DIY ancient Egyptian style!

Remember the whole "sleeping on the roof" thing?

Well, there were beds for some people — the ones who could afford it. But they weren't exactly what you'd call cosy.

You know something's wrong when you get splinters from your pillow.

They were made from wooden frames with a base of reeds. What was that? **PILLOWS?** Pillows indeed! The Egyptians didn't go in for all that **SUPER-SOFT NONSENSE**. Nope, they had wooden head-rests for pillows. That's right — **LOVELY, COMFORTABLE WOOD.**

Have a nice sleep!

Do you ever wish . . .
you didn't have to climb all those stairs to bed when you're soooo tired?

Well, at least there aren't as many steps as there are on the Great Pyramid at Giza. Khufu's Great Pyramid is the biggest stone building in the world. It is 146 metres (479 ft) high and is made from nearly 2.5 million blocks of limestone!

Although it looks worn and crumbled today, the Great Pyramid at Giza was once faced with gleaming white limestone and may even have been capped with gold! Makes your house seem a bit dull, doesn't it?

CHORES AND JOBS

Life can be SO unfair sometimes. There you are, hard at work annoying your sister, playing *Evil Zombie Brainsuckers 2* on your console or picking your nose when your mum rocks up and asks you to do a chore.

A chore? **A CHORE?** Can't you see I'm **UNBELIEVABLY BUSY** here, Mother? Noses don't pick themselves, you know!

But for some reason she won't listen and you have to spend **LITERALLY MINUTES** emptying the dishwasher.

That might sound **UNBEARABLE**, but if you think *YOU'VE* GOT IT BAD, get a load of this . . .

In ancient Egypt, children were gradually introduced to their parents' work from a much younger age than today.

As the majority of youngsters rarely attended school, there was plenty of time for them to get their hands dirty in the fields, at home and in the workshop.

FANCY THAT!
Men usually washed clothes in the river instead of women, because of the risk from crocodiles. And they had to be snappy about it!

At harvest time, men cut the crops with a sickle while women and children bound the stalks into sheaves. So **STOP MOANING** about taking the bins out.

Both boys and girls are depicted doing simple farm work in ancient drawings. A picture in the tomb of Djeserkareseneb (try saying that with a mouth full of custard!) shows a boy and girl beside each other picking up ears of corn, which they then put in a basket to carry.

It wasn't a great job, but at least you could freak people out by telling them that you were carrying a basket **FULL OF EARS**, which is pretty cool.

Do you ever wish . . .
you didn't have to tidy your room to earn pocket money?

Well, at least you get SOMETHING! In ancient Egypt, slaves were used to carry out work, serve households and build things.

Although slavery is shocking to us now, it was common back then. Many of the slaves were soldiers from other countries who had lost in battle to the Egyptians, and had been taken prisoner. Others had been sold into slavery.

Slaves even worked as musicians, dancers and accountants. Although it was once said that many thousands of slaves were used to build the pyramids, it is now thought that they weren't built by slaves at all, but by free men.

The people who owned slaves, called masters, could make an enslaved person learn a trade or craft. That wasn't to help them, though, it was to make the slave more valuable. One (very) small relief was that masters were not allowed to force child slaves to perform harsh physical jobs. But still, life wasn't exactly a hoot for slave kids . . .

Why? Because it's all ears?!

This basket is a great listener.

Some jobs for ancient Egyptian kids were divided between girls and boys.

Boys were often given the job of watching flocks or tending cattle, which sounds like it could be quite **HEAVY ON THE POO SIDE OF THINGS.**

A picture in one tomb shows a boy chasing birds away from a heap of grain, which could be a common chore for a young lad.

Of course, it was all **FINE AND DANDY** if the birds were cheeky little sparrows, but if an ostrich was having a nibble at your grain, he'd be the one doing the chasing.

PECK!
PECK!

As far as anyone is aware, however, there are no pictures in tombs of boys having their bottoms pecked by angry ostriches, so it must have been a rare occurrence.

3 YEARS OLD
Boys vs girls

Shopping

Feeding animals

7 YEARS OLD
Boys vs girls

Digging

FANCY THAT!

Eating gritty bread wore down people's teeth, because the flour usually had sand in it. Now that's what you call a SANDwich!

Girls were less likely to do jobs like these. They tended to help their mothers doing household chores such as cooking, sewing, making bread and the like, which are **BLISSFULLY POO-FREE** (hopefully).

However, they may also have been servants for rich families and royalty. Lucky **LITTLE PRINCE POSHPANTS** wouldn't have had any bird-chasing jobs on his to-do list. In the upper classes, it would have been slaves or servants who performed minor chores.

In one image from the time a servant girl arranges cushions on a chair while another smooths down bedsheets. It's bad enough having to make your own bed, so imagine having to do it for **SOMEONE ELSE. BARBARIC!**

Cooking

12 YEARS OLD
Boys vs girls

Farming

Babysitting

Here's a handy pyramid that shows who were the top of the pops job-wise, and who did the tough tasks at the bottom end.

Just call me the Head Honcho, guys!

PHARAOH

The Big Cheese. The Top Dog. Numero Uno. The people of Egypt believed that their pharaohs — or kings — were gods, and you can't get much higher than that. All powerful.

HIGH OFFICIALS

Even pharaohs need help sometimes, so they appointed top officials, such as a chief minister called a "vizier" who watched over tax collection and important records. The big guy's right-hand man.

I am so totally the best at throwing pointy things.

FARMERS

Just like today farmers tended the fields and raised animals for food and work. Although they weren't high in the social pyramid, their job was important. A tractor or two would have come in handy, mind you.

Anyone got a combine harvester for sale?

SOLDIERS

Soldiers fought wars and protected the country from invasion. They also supervised peasants and slaves during building projects. Carried pointy things, so best not messed with.

ARTISANS

Skilled workers made and sold jewellery, papyrus products, pottery, tools and suchlike. So if you're good at building things from little plastic bricks, maybe this would have been the job for you.

28

OMG! I can't believe you forgot your wig AGAIN!

NOBLES AND PRIESTS

If you came from a noble family, chances are your dad would have a job helping to run the country. Priests were responsible for pleasing the gods — the last thing anyone wanted was a grumpy god!

I hope no one notices I'm just doodling.

SCRIBES

Scribes were highly respected because they had a very handy skill: they could read and write, which meant they could keep government records. The fact that you're reading this book means you're already pretty scribey.

SERVANTS AND SLAVES

Life was tough at the bottom of the heap. Prisoners of war became slaves and were forced to work very hard for the pharaoh or nobles. You really wouldn't want to be at this end of the pyramid.

We're doing a great buy-one-get-one-free deal on magic charms today!

MERCHANTS

They bought goods from artisans and then sold them to the public. It would be handy to come from a merchant family — first choice on all the best amulets and wooden pillows!

29

EDUCATION

When was the last time you saw a dog with a schoolbag?
Or heard a cat grumbling about having to do homework?

NEVER, that's when. Because animals have it easy.

You, on the other hand, have to get up at SILLY O'CLOCK in the morning, PUT ON A SCHOOL UNIFORM and go off to have your brain STUFFED WITH FACTS.

But if you think *YOU'VE* GOT IT BAD . . . you're very much mistaken.

No girls allowed!

Would it help if we grew beards?

FANCY THAT!
Formal schooling was mostly for the boys of wealthier families. Girls only rarely had an education outside of the home, which seems pretty unfair.

Although historians know many things about ancient Egypt, funnily enough, not a lot is known about how schools were organised as there are no pictures of schools from the time.

However, it's likely most were held in the open air.

That sounds like fun in a hot country like Egypt.

But while it might have been nice and warm, it was also a bit, you know, CROCODILE-Y . . .

> Hey! Where's Mahu? He was at the back of the class a minute ago.

> That's odd. It's just that new kid with the green scaly skin and big mouth who's there now . . .

Do you ever wish . . .
that you didn't have to take the school bus?

Would you prefer to catch a boat to school? Sounds a bit soggy.

Most of ancient Egypt was based along the Nile, so boats and ferries were one of the most popular ways of getting around.

Donkeys were used a lot for carrying heavy loads, and donkey trains were used as well as boats. A donkey train is like a steam train but with less steam and more legs.

Horses and chariots weren't common at all in the early times of ancient Egypt. When chariots did arrive, they were used for hunting and in wars. They were made of wood and leather, and were popular with rich people who wanted to flash the cash.

What about camels, you ask? Forget about it! Camels did not appear in Egypt until much later.

But the most common way to get around was... guess? Yes! Those things at the end of your legs. Most folk travelled everywhere on foot.

We're sorry to reveal there were no bicycles.

SOLDIER

For most ancient Egyptian kids who weren't royal or rich, much of their education was carried out by their fathers.

POTTER

And it wouldn't have included lessons in the way you know them. It was more a case of passing on knowledge about Dad's craft or skill.

TAILOR

JEWELLER

The sons of royal families, high officials and nobles could go to the Prince's School, the most respected school in the land. It taught reading and writing, history, mathematics, geography, astronomy, medicine and **SKATEBOARDING SKILLS** (it's **VERY** hard to ride a skateboard in the desert without proper training, you see).

There were certainly no class projects on ancient Egypt! Back then ancient Egypt was just, well, **EGYPT**.

SCULPTOR

Some schools were there to teach children to do particular jobs when they were older, such as being a scribe. They were the people who could read and write hieroglyphs and had the task of documenting Egyptian life.

Is it wrong that there's more ink on me than the papyrus?

Most of what we know about ancient Egypt is thanks to the work of scribes, so they were **VERY** important.

Fancy being a scribe? Well, students would spend **HOURS AND HOURS** writing and re-writing the hundreds of signs that made up words.

Hey, **COME BACK!**

I **THOUGHT** you wanted to be a scribe?

FANCY THAT!
Scribes wrote letters on papyrus rolls, using reed brushes and ink made with soot. You're probably best sticking to felt tips instead.

Do you ever wish . . . you were better at painting?

Well at least you aren't expected to paint a whole tomb ... which sounds a bit on the spooky side, as well as hard work.

A lot of what we know nowadays about the lives of the ancient Egyptians is thanks to the work of artists and scribes, who painted pictures or drew hieroglyphs.

Painting a tomb took a lot of work. First a stonemason smoothed the wall and covered it with plaster and a grid was made using red paint. Then an outline scribe transferred sketches to the grid with black paint. Next a stonemason chipped out the main figures, before finally a painter filled in the background and added flesh tones.

Sounds a bit more heavy going than art class in school.

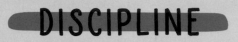

DISCIPLINE

If you ever get your hands on *The Bumper Book Of Being A Grown-Up* (every adult has one, but is sworn to keep it a secret from children), turn to page 437.

In the chapter titled "99 Terrible Punishments for Annoyingly Naughty Kids" it lists the various ways grown-ups can make your life a **MISERY** if you **STEP OUT OF LINE**.

Here's a small selection:

- Brussels sprouts for tea every night for a month.
- No sweets for a year.
- Glue them to a cow (only for extreme naughtiness).
- Chores. So, so many chores. Mwa-ha-haaa!

You've probably suffered at least one of those awful fates.

But if you think *YOU'VE* GOT IT BAD, think again.

It could be worse . . .

CHEEKY DRAWING

In ancient Egyptian times, discipline was a **LITTLE HARSHER** than it is today.

Come back here!

I'd really rather not, if you don't mind!

Kids were never made to simply sit on the naughty step of a pyramid when they were badly behaved.

In school, if you got into trouble for doodling, you could be in for a **VERY NASTY** surprise!

Teachers treated troublemaking seriously and punishments for pupils included **WRITING OUT LINES** and even being **BEATEN WITH A STICK!**

Do you ever wish . . .
your teacher would give you a break?

At least the worst you can expect is a letter home to your parents. Punishments could be very strict in ancient Egyptian schools. One ancient Egyptian proverb reads:

> "A boy's ear is on his back;
> he hears when he is beaten."

So that's doubly bad news. First you have ears on your back, which is just weird and means it's very difficult to hear when you're wearing a jumper. And then your scary teacher bops your back-ears with a big stick to help you learn!

But it's not my fault the dog ate my homework!

If you think the punishments in lessons sound bad . . .

. . . even if you were playing games with your pals, if you broke the rules the punishment could be **A BOP ON THE NOSE, A SHARP KICK OR TWO** or even being **TIED UP AND THRASHED**.

Not exactly your average game of rounders.

Sob!

Perhaps we should stick to Monopoly from now on?

GROSS KEBAB

For really bad peeps there were some pretty **GRUESOME** punishments around that were guaranteed to stop them being bad ever again — mainly due to them being **A BIT ON THE DEAD SIDE**.

It has been claimed that some criminals were fed to **CROCODILES**, though this should probably be taken with a pinch of salt (the claim, not the criminals — crocs don't like salt).

But the worst punishment was being impaled on a big wooden stake. **EEEUW!** It's enough to put you off kebabs for life.

Quick! Catch that dangerous criminal, police monkey!

How about the dog takes a turn for a change?

Someone had to keep an eye out for ancient naughtiness, so there were policemen armed with staffs guarding public places. They also had dogs, and it's even thought they may even have used **TRAINED MONKEYS** to help them catch bad guys.

It's unlikely you'll ever see that kind of thing happen nowadays, but if you ever spot a police car being driven by a **VERY SMALL, HAIRY POLICEMAN EATING A BANANA**, you'll know the cops are trying out some ancient Egyptian ideas.

DIET

We've all had one of "those" meals — you know, the one you still have nightmares about on dark stormy nights.

It usually happens on a visit to an elderly relative.

"Here, have some of this," says Great Auntie Ethel.
"Err, what is it?" you stammer.
"Jellied cow tongue with kidney gravy and cold boiled spinach."
THUD-bleeeuuuurrgghh-thumpthumpthump
(That's the sound of you **FAINTING**, **BEING SICK** and then **RUNNING AWAY**.)

But if you think *YOU'VE* **GOT IT BAD**, wrap your peepers around these ancient Egyptian foody favourites...

> Pass the grapes, please!

> Oh, what's for dinner? Fish or more fish?

FISH

BEER

BREAD

Most poorer Egyptians sat on the floor to eat, using their fingers. See what your mum says if you try **THAT** at dinner tonight.

It's pretty much guaranteed that whatever nasties you've ever eaten, nothing matches some of the delicacies that the ancient Egyptians used to enjoy such as **PIGEONS** and **GAZELLES!**

DO NOT adjust your eyes: you read that right.

Needless to say, pigeons and gazelles weren't the **STANDARD TYPES OF GRUB** for most ancient Egyptians. The staple diet of both the rich and poor was based on bread, vegetables and fish, and depending how wealthy the family was, meat and poultry.

Guess what's for dessert . . . fish!

CAT
(NOT FOOD)

DATES

MORE FISH

GRAPES

FANCY THAT!
One tomb painting suggests that rich ancient Egyptians even fattened up hyenas to be eaten at feasts. That's no laughing matter!

39

And what did Egyptian children (and grown-ups) wash down their dinner with? Beer of course!

That's right, even the **KIDS** drank beer back in those days!

FANCY THAT!

Almost everyone in ancient Egypt loved eating garlic and onions, while ostrich eggs were a great treat. Kisses must have been a bit on the pongy side.

The Egyptian beer was **NOTHING** like the kind drunk by adults today, though. It was thick and probably sweet, with nutritious solids floating in it. More like gruel. **YUMMY**.

Best sticking to orange squash, don't you think?

The poor would certainly have eaten more basic foods than the rich enjoyed. When normal families ate meat it would tend to be from sheep or goats.

Beef was usually more expensive and would mainly have been scoffed by royalty. So if you're **NOT** related to the Queen, I'm afraid you'll have to put down that beefburger. Here's a tasty goatburger instead. **ENJOY!**

Do you ever wish . . . you could have something other than cornflakes or toast and jam for breakfast?

Well, instead of complaining in that annoying voice, you should thank your lucky stars that you don't have to put up with what a poor person in ancient Egypt would start the day with. Get this — back then peasants would probably have eaten a simple breakfast of bread and onions.

Yep, you heard. Onions. For brekkie.

Good luck not having totally stinky breath for the rest of the day.

And if that's not bad enough, try tossing garlic into the mix.

According to the Greek historian Herodotus, the pyramids were constructed by workers whose main foods were garlic, radishes and onions. Garlic, which was eaten plain or used as a flavouring, has even been found in tombs, including Tutankhamun's. Pooh! You'd have to put a peg on your nose just to have a conversation with each other without fainting.

If onion and garlic weren't to your liking, and you were very rich, you could always eat a cow. As in the whole thing. In those days all parts of the animal would be chomped . . . including most of the internal organs.

So if you like the sound of a little nibble on a heart for supper or a nice kidney sandwich for lunch, ancient Egypt would be right up your gross street.

You may want to stick to garlic. Or cornflakes.

Upper class families and royalty often enjoyed banquets, waited on by slaves and servants.

I couldn't possibly eat any more. I've already had two pigeon burgers and a goose pizza.

Dancers and musicians playing harps, drums and tambourines entertained the diners, who were able to tuck into **VAST** quantities of food.

Scented cones of grease were placed on people's heads during banquets. As they melted a nice smell was released as it dripped over wigs and clothes. (You may want to avoid trying this out at your school disco.)

Ewww. What's that funky smell?

I knew I shouldn't have gone for the cheese and onion hair cone.

FANCY THAT!
Rich Egyptians liked to eat raw cabbage as a starter at meals. How much do you now NOT want to be a rich ancient Egyptian?

There were whole roast oxen (think cow), geese, ducks and pigeons. And afterwards came the cakes — yes, even the ancient Egyptians loved a nice bit of cake.

But don't get too excited at the sound of **ALL THAT LOVELY GRUB**. Unless you currently live in **A CASTLE**, you're **NOT** the sort who'd get your mitts on that kind of dinner.

Now eat up — you've **HARDLY** touched your raw cabbage.

43

HEALTH AND MEDICINE

Going to the doctors isn't usually a fun day out. First you sit in the waiting room while people sneeze on the back of your head . . .

Then you're **POKED** and **PRODDED** by the doc, who peers in your ears and up your nose with one of those funny torch things.

Finally, it is decided that the best way to get the saucepan off your head is to smear your noggin with butter and get two people to pull your legs and two to pull the saucepan.

It's **HARDLY** relaxing.

But if you think *YOU'VE* GOT IT BAD, just wait till you hear this . . .

> I'm pretty sure I'm meant to have five fingers.

> If anyone's planning on going fishing then I have some worms in my leg you can have.

Ancient Egyptians had plenty of reasons to visit a doc: from natural diseases and worms which **LAID EGGS** in their legs, to nasty accidents or run-ins with dangerous animals like **HIPPOS**, **CROCODILES** and **SCORPIONS**.

Poorer people had to make do with a local person with limited medical knowledge.

Better-off people had access to doctors who, like modern medics, asked questions about what was wrong, took the patient's pulse and examined the part of the body that was affected.

But what happened when you were inside the surgery?

Once the doc worked out what was causing the problem — perhaps you'd been **CHOMPED IN TWO** by an **ANGRY CROCODILE**, for instance, and were feeling **A LITTLE** under the weather — they could work out what treatment to offer.

It's only Cow-poo-pol. Drink up!

Now I REALLY feel ill!

BIRD BLOOD

But unlike today, there were no handy pills from the chemist.

Back then treatments may have used spices such as cinnamon or pepper or less appealing ingredients such as mud or dung. So next time you see a cow pat, pop it in your pocket — it might come in handy when you're feeling a bit dodgy.

HONEY AND SALT

Another treatment included the blood of a bird, flies' blood, honey and salt.

COW PAT

PEPPER

Errr, thanks, Doc . . . suddenly we feel MUCH better. No need for medicine after all. BYEEE!

FLY BLOOD

Not all Egyptian remedies were medical. They believed in the power of magic and spells as well.

Of course, if the blood, dung and magic didn't cure you, you might end up **SLIGHTLY ON THE DEAD SIDE**.

SHAAZZZZAMMM!!

Nice try, but the verruca's still there.

FANCY THAT!

Mothers sometimes ate a mouse to try to cure sick children. They would then put the bones in a bag tied with seven knots and hang it around the child's neck for good luck. Please do not try this at home to try to cure a sniffle.

Do you ever wish . . . you didn't have to get injections?

Well, of course no one enjoys getting pointy things stuck in them (unless they're REALLY weird) — but usually it's done to take away pain or give you medicine that actually works.

Back in the day, you wouldn't have had an injection to take away the pain — because such things didn't exist. You just had to grin and bear it. Or, rather, scream and bear it.

And as for giving you medicine that works, well try this on for size . . . an ancient text reveals the recipe for a "cure" for blindness. Here it is:

"A pig's eye, antimony [a powdered metal], red ochre [a powdered red colouring] and a little honey are finely ground and mixed together and poured into the ear of the man so that he may be

cured at once. Then recite this spell twice: 'I have brought this ointment and applied it to the trouble spot and it will remove the horrible suffering'. A really excellent remedy."

Yes, excellent. Except pouring mushed-up pig's eyes and honey into someone's ear definitely does NOT cure blindness. It just gunks up their ear with totally gross gunge.

In any case, if you don't like needles, don't worry — Egyptian docs didn't have them. Instead they used knives, hooks, drills, forceps, pincers, spoons, saws and even fire.

Suddenly getting a tiny little jab in the behind doesn't seem quite so bad now, does it?

If there was one thing the ancient Egyptians knew about, it was prepping the dead for the afterlife.

We're talking MUMMIES.

The entire process took 70 DAYS.

STEP 1

First the internal organs — except the heart and kidneys — were removed through a hole cut in the left side.

Ready, steady, SCOOP!

BRAIN SCOOPY STICK

STEP 2

The brain was then scooped out through the nose and chucked away.

IMPORTANT NOTE!

If you see an ancient Egyptian coming towards you with a teaspoon and a glint in his eye, either run away or hold your nose.

The organs were dried, wrapped and placed in containers called CANOPIC JARS.

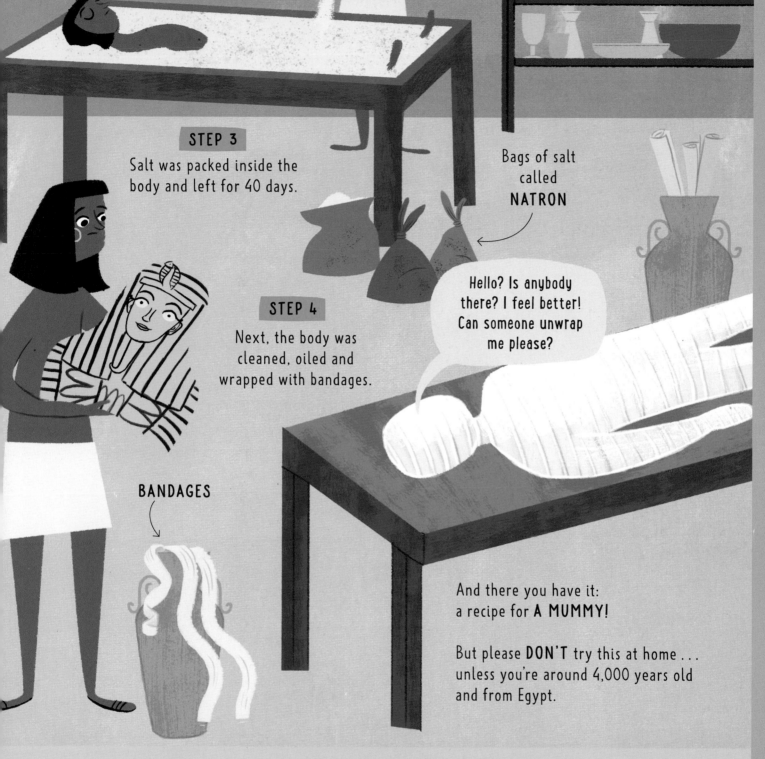

STEP 3

Salt was packed inside the body and left for 40 days.

Bags of salt called **NATRON**

STEP 4

Next, the body was cleaned, oiled and wrapped with bandages.

Hello? Is anybody there? I feel better! Can someone unwrap me please?

BANDAGES

And there you have it: a recipe for **A MUMMY!**

But please **DON'T** try this at home . . . unless you're around 4,000 years old and from Egypt.

Do you ever wish . . . you could be turned into a mummy?

Probably not, so it's just as well you don't live in ancient Egypt.

The poor weren't important (or rich) enough to get the full "bandage him up and stick him in a pyramid" treatment like kings and officials did, but it was still important for their body to be preserved for the afterlife, so they were buried in the desert where the sand dried them out.

Tools, food and jewellery were buried alongside them for use in the afterlife. Wealthy folk had their bodies wrapped up — the "full mummy" (as it wasn't known) — and their possessions placed alongside them in proper tombs.

Hey, this all seems a bit, you know, "deady"... so let's move on.

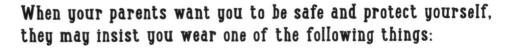

GODS, AMULETS AND PROTECTION

When your parents want you to be safe and protect yourself, they may insist you wear one of the following things:

1. A bicycle helmet.
2. Knee and elbow pads for skateboarding.
3. A waterproof jacket.
4. A bodysuit made entirely from bubble-wrap (if they're **REALLY** cautious).

But don't grumble — if you think *YOU'VE* GOT IT BAD there were things in ancient Egypt that kids really **DID** need protection from . . . because knee pads and an anorak wouldn't be much use if a croc decided the main course for lunch was "kid surprise".

Whether it was being gobbled up by **HUNGRY HIPPOS**, falling into the Nile, being stung by **STINGY THINGIES** or coming down with a **DREADFUL DISEASE** that made your head **SWELL UP** like a beach ball and your **BOTTOM FALL OFF**, there was certainly a lot for mums and dads to worry about back then.

So it's not surprising ancient Egyptians worshipped gods and used protective amulets to help keep their children safe.

FANCY THAT!
Blue was the "sky colour", and people thought it was lucky. So if your dad asks why you've dyed your hair blue, now you have a good reason.

People back then had hundreds of gods to choose from. Gods were often pictured with animal heads to help identify them and to show their special quality.

The most important of them was the sun-god, Ra.

Osiris was the god of the dead and had green skin! People believed he helped their ancestors plant crops, bake bread and make wine, which was nice of him.

The chief goddess, Isis, was married to her own brother Osiris (aaawkwaaard).

Horus, the god of the sky and son of Isis and Osiris (still aaawkwaaard), had the head of a falcon.

The goddess Sakhmet the Powerful had the head of a lioness.

The goddess Taueret had a crocodile head, a hippo's body and a lion's legs. Now that's what you call a mash-up.

FETCH!

IMPORTANT NOTE!
As far as we know there were no gods with the head of a hamster, goldfish or bumblebee.

Anubis, who was the god of mummification, had the head of a jackal, a type of wild dog.

A little help from the gods . . .

He's pretty weird . . . but I kinda like him.

Not all of the gods had animal heads. One of the most popular, **BES**, had the head of . . . **ERRR**, a beardy, cheeky, little guy with his tongue poking half way down his whiskery chinny-chin-chin.

(No, we are **NOT** totally making this stuff up.)

RATTLE TO SCARE OFF SNAKES

LION'S TAIL

Bes wasn't the god of **WILD PARTY DUDES** who like sticking their tongues out at people — although that does sound like a pretty cool kind of god. In fact, the ancient Egyptians turned to him for protection when a baby was being born and he helped ward off bad spirits, so he was very important.

BOW LEGS

Check out my cool wand, bro.

Another lucky charm was a wand made from hippopotamus tusk (not quite **SO** lucky for the hippo, of course). It was decorated with hieroglyphs and was said to protect a child from being bitten by poisonous beasties with big pointy teeth as they slept.

Next time you're worried you're about to be stung by a wasp, just **WAGGLE A HIPPO WAND** in its direction. That'll teach it!

Sigh. I suppose this means I can't eat you?

People in Egypt also believed lucky charms called amulets protected them and their children from harm.

Better safe than sorry!

Uh, Mummy? I can't ACTUALLY move!

For instance, a fish amulet worn at the end of a braid of a child's hair would protect them from drowning in the Nile or being eaten by crocodiles.

IMPORTANT NOTE!

Do not try gluing a sardine to your head and getting all up in a croc's face — it will NOT work.

Do you ever wish . . .
you could speak a secret language?

Well, perhaps if you took some time out of your busy schedule of playing video games and picking your nose and tried to learn a bit about hieroglyphics, you could be getting all secret with your best buddies sooner rather than later.

First things first: the word hieroglyph isn't even Egyptian. It's Greek for "sacred writing", just to confuse you.

And while there might be 26 letters in the English alphabet, the ancient Egyptians would laugh their wigs off at that puny letter-count. Their hieroglyphic system used a total of around 900 different signs!

Hey! Come back! You don't have to learn all 900 now.

OK, take a breath, chill out, and give this a go for starters. Put on your thinking cap — and your creativity pants — and have a go at drawing your own hieroglyphs.

Try translating this sentence into your own made-up language:

"MY BEST FRIEND DOES HUGE BOTTOM-BURPS THAT SOUND LIKE A GIANT PLAYING AN OLD TUBA AND SMELL LIKE ROTTEN EGGS, CABBAGE AND STINKY SOCKS."

How did you get on? Excellent! You'd fit right in back in ancient Egypt.

OTHER WORDS WRITTEN IN HIEROGLYPHS

CROCODILE

MUMMY

CAT

Thoth, the god of knowledge and writing was sometimes shown as an ibis or a baboon. Trying to get a real ibis to write may disappoint.

FUN AND GAMES

Well, here we are at the end of our journey to ancient Egypt. But we wouldn't want you to go away thinking it was all wooden pillows, scorpions and unpleasant punishments.

Even though Egyptian kids had plenty on their plates — delicious pigeon kebabs, for instance — there was still time to enjoy the more entertaining side of life.

So if you think *THEY* had it bad, **THEY DIDN'T!**

Well, not **ALL** the time . . .

Hmmm. Which bottom shall I bite first?

You'd better be a good swimmer . . .

If there's one thing people associate with Egypt — apart from pyramids and mummies — it's the River Nile. So it's not surprising it featured strongly in children's leisure time, with swimming, boating and river games among their favourite activities.

It must have been excellent training for swimming quickly, too. Well, wouldn't you do the front crawl **PRETTY SPEEDILY** if you had a **TOOTHY CROC** or a **HUNGRY HIPPO** snapping at your behind?

Do you ever wish . . . you could go to the swimming pool more often?

Well, at least when you do there are no crocodiles or hippos following you around. (And if there are, you should really tell a lifeguard.)

Sport was enjoyed by many in ancient Egypt, and not surprisingly, given the presence of the Nile, swimming was one of their favourite pastimes — although it was always necessary to keep an eye out for bitey things.

Wrestling was also big — but not the spangly-shorts-jumping-off-the-ropes kind, this was more serious. Mind you, some famous Middle Kingdom tomb paintings show boys lifting each other off the ground and even holding each other upside-down!

Inscriptions on monuments reveal that the ancient Egyptians also took part in the likes of weightlifting, long jumping, rowing, fishing and acrobatics.

Sounds like you'd be fit as a fiddle if you lived back then. Definitely no lounging around playing the games console in those days . . .

There was a lot of fun to be had in ancient Egypt . . .

The sunny climate was ideal for outdoor games such as leapfrog, tug of war and acrobatics. Just like today, ball games were popular. The balls were made out of papyrus or leather with straw stuffing.

TUG OF WAR

LEAPFROG

There was no football back then, so don't bother looking for hieroglyphs about a game between **SANDCHESTER UNITED** and **TUTANKHAMUN HOTSPUR**, because you won't find 'em.

JUGGLING

Instead, juggling was **THE IN THING**. If you know any clowns with a time machine, tell them to get back there pronto — they'll be a **BIG** hit.

One ancient painting even depicts **A MOUSE JUGGLING!**

Sadly, the amazing juggling mice of ancient Egypt must have died out — presumably they were eaten in a sandwich.

Girls were also pictured passing balls to each other while riding piggyback on a partner, which sounds fun if you were the ones doing the passing, but **NOT SO MUCH** if you were the ones doing the carrying.

ACROBATICS

In one game, called the Star Game, two boys stood in the middle holding two other friends with outstretched arms.

Then they'd spin their pals around as fast as they could.

CARTWHEEL

OK, it's not exactly high-tech, but you have to admit it sounds like fun. Until you **SPIN INTO A PYRAMID**, of course. **OUCH.**

THE STAR GAME

Do you ever wish . . . you had more music to stream on your phone?

Well, at least you can take music with you in your pocket. In ancient Egypt things weren't so mobile.

Music was very important as a form of entertainment and also in worshipping gods. Instruments included harps, drums, rattles, cymbals, tambourines, flutes, clarinets, double pipes and trumpets.

The Egyptians didn't write their music down so no-one knows what it sounded like — although we can safely say it probably didn't resemble an **EAR-BLASTING HEAVY-METAL CONCERT.**

So be glad you don't need to take a full band with you everywhere just to listen to your fave album.

Wow! You win again, Tut. What a surprise!

Yeah, probably just as well, what with me being king and all.

We all like a good board game, and the ancient Egyptians were no different.

They didn't have Monopoly or Cluedo though, they had a game called Senet.

It was played by members of the royal families, including Tutankhamun. We're guessing his pals let him win **EVERY** time, just in case.

To play the game, each player rolled a dice and would move their pieces around and eventually off the board while trying to stop their opponents doing the same thing with their pieces.

It may be hard to picture from several thousand years away, but it's likely that at some point somebody **CHEATED**, someone else went off **IN A HUFF**, someone **ACCIDENTALLY KNOCKED ALL THE PIECES OFF THE BOARD** because they were mucking around, and finally everyone was sent to bed by Mum and Dad . . .

NOTHING CHANGES.

STILL THINK YOU'VE GOT IT BAD?

Well, we hope you've enjoyed your tour of ancient Egypt. Now you have to ask yourself one very important question — do you STILL think YOU'VE GOT IT BAD?

YOU DO? REALLY?

So you regularly find **SCORPIONS IN YOUR PANTS** and have to **DODGE CROCODILES** hanging around your garden pond?

You have **PIGEON PIZZA** for school dinner?

You worry about having your **BRAINS SCOOPED OUT** through your nose and flung in the bin?

HAAAANG ON . . . you're talking hippo poop, aren't you?

You know fine well that those poor ancient Egyptian kids had it a **WHOLE LOT WORSE** than you in many ways — although if you're a fan of sand or being slightly bald then you may have thought it was a right old hoot.

This job stinks!

Yikes! That hippo looks hungry!

Help! Another stingy thingy!

Because while you might be fed up with some of the things you have to put up with today, if you think you've got it bad . . . **you really don't!**

GLOSSARY

This may come as a surprise to you, but there were NO SKATEBOARDS or BUBBLE WRAP in ancient Egypt. SORRY TO DISAPPOINT, but that's just how it was.

We also don't know if kids really had to shovel dung — but we imagine it was very possible, what with all the cows running around . . . and we couldn't LEAVE OUT THE POO now could we? Other than that, the facts in this book are accurate. So if you sort of ignore the bits about MICROWAVES and MOBILES, you might just learn a thing or two about ancient Egypt!

AFTERLIFE

When someone died, ancient Egyptians believed their soul would go on a journey — first to the Underworld, which was a scary and dangerous place, and then into the Field of Rushes, which was a place of great peace and bliss. It was important the soul didn't get distracted along the way and end up going to the cinema or having a burger at the shopping mall. Straight to the afterlife, soul — no mucking around. Right?

AMULET

An ornament or small piece of jewellery thought to give protection against evil, danger or disease. Just in case you were wondering, a small plastic moustache from a Christmas cracker doesn't count as an amulet and will NOT protect you from being chomped by an angry hippopotamus.

ARCHAEOLOGIST

A person who studies human history and prehistory by digging ancient sites and studying artefacts and other physical and human remains found there (we're talking skeletons, peeps). You can practise by burying your dad's slippers in the garden and then digging them up again. Just don't tell him we suggested that when you can't find them . . .

CANOPIC JARS

Covered urns used in ancient Egyptian burials to hold the entrails and other internal organs from an embalmed body. Great fun at parties if you want to play a game of "What's in the Jar?" — just pop your hand in the urn, have a rummage around the slippery stuff and try to guess if it's kidneys or lungs. What a hoot! Winner gets a spoonful of brains to take home.

HIEROGLYPHS

The Egyptian writing called hieroglyphs or hieroglyphics used around 900 pictures, signs and symbols to represent different objects, actions, sounds and ideas. Just one problem — we've checked and checked and we just can't find the symbol for fart (or bottom-burp). Surely there's been a mistake. How on earth could you get by without that? Impossible!

KHUFU

Khufu was a pharaoh of the 4th Dynasty (around 4,500 years ago) who ordered the Great Pyramid of Giza to be built to hold his tomb. It's one of the Seven Wonders of the Ancient World. He also ordered the Medium-sized Shed of Giza to be built, followed by the Little Tree House of Giza, but no-one ever talks about those these days.

MIDDLE KINGDOM

This is the period in the history of ancient Egypt between around 2050 BC (which was more than 4,000 years ago) and 1800 BC, beginning with the reunification of Egypt under Mentuhotep II. During this time, all of Egypt was united under one government and pharaoh. Sounds like the dudes were pretty chilled out and chummy at this point. Sweet.

MUMMY

The body of an important person, such as a pharaoh, that has been ceremonially preserved by removing the internal organs, then treated with natron (see top of next page) and resin and wrapped in bandages. Please do not try doing that to your own mummy — or daddy for that matter — especially if you are hoping for a pocket money raise any time in the next 100 years.

NATRON

Natron was a salt mixture harvested from dry lake beds. Blended with oil, it was an early form of soap and was used to prepare bodies for mummification. If you ever get asked to prepare a pharaoh for mummification, remember to use natron and not your bubblegum-scented shampoo.

PAPYRUS

This is a material similar to thick paper that was used in ancient times to write on. It was made from the pith of the papyrus plant, which was found growing all around the Nile. Just think — if this book was around back then, it could have been made from plants found within a snickety-snap of a crocodile's teeth. That's what you call a book with bite!

PYRAMID

The ancient Egyptians built pyramids as tombs for the pharaohs and their queens. The pharaohs were buried in pyramids of many different shapes and sizes, the biggest of which was the Great Pyramid of Giza. It took 10-20 years to be built by tens of thousands of workers — some say as many as 200,000! So if you're planning to build one in your garden, you'd better have plenty of pals.

RAMESES II

Rameses II — also known as Rameses the Great — was one of the greatest pharaohs ever. He signed the world's first official peace treaty, had many great buildings constructed, reigned for over 67 years . . . and is said to have had more than 100 children! Imagine trying to get into the bathroom before all those brothers and sisters on a school day! Stressful or what?

SENET

A board game that was a favourite among ancient Egyptians. The full name of the game in Egyptian is thought to mean the "game of passing". It was a game of strategy, a little like chess. And no, you can't get *Senet 2: Revenge of the Pharaoh* on the PlayStation. Although it does sound pretty good. Hey! It's our idea! Hands off!

SICKLE

A short-handled farming tool with a semi-circular blade, used for cutting corn, lopping, or trimming. This is what ancient Egyptian farmers would have used to cut crops. It was very unusual to see a combine harvester on the banks of the Nile. Or even a small tractor. They were all about the sickles, those ancient Egyptians. Loved a good sickle.

TOMB

A chamber that is used as a grave. Tombs could stand alone, or they could be built into the heart of a pyramid, with sealed passages leading into them. Over the centuries tombs were often raided by robbers looking for treasure. Do you fancy poking around a dark tomb in the dead of night next to a dusty mummy? Nope? Well best not apply for a job as an ancient Egyptian tomb robber then.

TUTANKHAMUN

Tutankhamun was the 11th pharaoh of the 18th dynasty. He is probably the most famous pharaoh of them all, mainly due to the discovery of his perfectly preserved tomb by the British archaeologist Howard Carter in 1922. Tutankhamun was about 17 when he died and probably inherited the throne at the age of eight or nine. Now you know what to demand for your next birthday — a huge golden throne and immense power over an entire country. Make it so, parents!

VIZIER

The job of vizier in ancient Egypt was very important. In fact, he was the pharaoh's right-hand man. They were essentially the ones who ran the country, making sure everything went smoothly, so they had to be super-organised. If you struggle to keep your bedroom floor free of smelly socks and stinky pants and regularly drop your homework down the toilet, you'd probably find being a vizier a bit of a stretch.

INDEX

Afterlife 48-49, 62
Amulets 50-53, 62
Archaeologists 7, 62
Artisans 28
Banquets 42-43
Beer 40
Bes 52
Blue 50
Boats 31
Bread 12, 27
Brothers 10, 12
Camels 31
Canopic jars 48, 62
Carvings 6
Cats 14, 15
Chariots 31
Climate 7, 17, 56
Clothes 6-8, 22, 42
Crocodiles 24, 37, 53
Crops 25
Discipline 34-37
Doctors 44-47
Dogs 15, 37
Donkeys 31
Education 30-33
Farmers 28
Food 38-43
Furniture 22-23
Games 56-58
Garlic 40, 41
Gods 29, 50-53
Gold 23
Hairstyles 8-9
Harvest 25
Herodotus 41
Hieroglyphs 33, 52, 53, 62
High Officials 28
Houses 17-23
Jobs 24-29, 33
Khufu 23, 62
King Rameses II 12, 15, 63
Limestone 17, 23
Magic 47
Medicine 46-47

Merchants 29
Middle Kingdom 8, 62
Mummies 11, 48-49, 62
Mummification 48-49, 51
Music 58
Natron 49, 63
Nobles 29
Onions 40, 41
Paintings 6, 8, 12, 25, 26, 33, 39, 56
Papyrus 33, 56, 63
Pets 14-15
Pharaohs 12, 28
Policemen 37
Priests 29
Prince's School 32
Pyramids 23, 41, 62, 63
Queen Hatshepshut 8
River Nile 24, 31, 55
Schoolbook 12
Scribes 29, 33
Senet 58-59, 63
Servants 7, 11, 27, 29, 42
Sickle 25, 63
Sisters 10, 12, 13
Slaves 19, 25, 27, 29, 42
Soldiers 25, 28
Special occasions 7
Spells 47, 48
Sport 55
Star Game 57
Swimming 55
The Book of the Dead 48
Toilets 19
Tomb of Djeserkareseneb 25
Tomb of Menna 13
Tombs 8, 13, 63
Tutankhamun 58, 63
Underpants 6
Vizier 28, 63
Water 18, 19
Wigs 9, 42
Women 11, 18, 25
Wrestling 55